PRAISE FOR SPEAKING OF BROKEN GLASS

The first thing I read on my Sabbatical was a poem from *Speaking of Broken Glass*—"Nap Time." Jordan's poetry immediately ministered to me, giving me permission to be honest with my weary soul. Throughout the book, Jordan's vulnerability and vivid imagery empowers the reader to be real with the difficulty of whole hearted discipleship, specifically our obsession with external validation through performance, productivity, positions, or popularity. The poetic truths in *Speaking of Broken Glass* will bind your heart and focus your faith on Jesus and the gospel, helping you shatter your alabaster jars in worship of Jesus. Jordan's work is an artful gift to every Christian searching for authenticity in their discipleship.

—**Pastor A. Mitchell Moore**, pastor and co-founder of *The Dwelling*.

CALLA PRESS
PUBLISHING

SPEAKING OF BROKEN GLASS

JORDAN SLEED

POETRY

To my wife, Jen, for living with the me that lags behind the intentions named in many of these poems, for loving me, and for opening my eyes to see that Love is the greatest.

CONTENTS

INTRODUCTION

I live in a world which often lives in me. A world marked by an insatiable hunger for success. Define that how you will: progress, benchmarks, achievements, proof of time well-spent, articulate stories tied together with neat beginnings and endings. In the end, it's more easily *felt* than defined. This hunger floats through the air, and so I breathe it in until I know only to salivate for the *arrival* which I trust will satisfy. I say I'm after improvement, after "*a life worthy of the calling*" (Ephesians 4:1) I've received. But rather than being permeated by peace and extending abundance, my heart reveals that my goals are not an extension of the gift of eternal life, but a means to my own survival. As if without each moving ideal being realized, I will surely die.

But the data is in: the incessant pursuit of progress, benchmarks, and measurable success does not lead to a life well-lived. What good does it do to gain the world if you lose your soul in the process? What if what you are pursuing with all your ambition, good ideas, and subconscious survivalism has already proven that it cannot offer back to you the vitality of life you desperately desire? We can recall famous examples of benchmarks met, or success achieved, that tell this story on a spotlight-saturated scale. Whether it's Tom Brady asking "Why do I have three Super Bowl rings and still think there's something greater out there for me?" or John D. Rockefeller, worth hundreds of billions, saying "just a little bit more" would be "enough", the stories aren't hard to find.

Psychologists have coined a wonderful phrase to describe this phenomenon: *the arrival fallacy*. It's everywhere, even though the achievements I've listed might give the appearance that this arrival fallacy is simply a problem for the rich and famous. This deceptive notion is fully capable of incapacitating any well-intentioned, thoughtful human being.

The reality is, whether I reach celebrity status or not, I cannot escape the pressure to meet certain "measurements" of success. Perhaps this is a result of nurture. After all, my father was a sports statistician. I've always had a mind for tracking and retaining information correlated to progress. Sometimes I anticipate the infographics that will be displayed after a long tennis rally or a basketball team on a run. These measurements are, more or less, harmless.

But many of the measurements I make are more subtle, more self-oriented, and more nagging. They are the measurements and projections that lead me to obsessively track my "spiritual growth" or my "purpose" being fulfilled. They present as a slight tension in my shoulders, pull me out of bed in the morning, and propel me into many tasks that are not, in and of themselves, bad. They are baptized and then monetized by the machines often created in the name of ministry. And I have, many times, participated in transferring their panic-driven idealism into the hearts and minds of others. Like the deceptive people described by the prophets and psalmists, I have often said I am "for peace" while truly being "for war".

It is the assumption that I am at *war* that drives me to obsessively seek after "arrival" at the right amount of success. The man who knows he has "peace with God" (Romans 5:1) does not live as though each day is a mission in which God has asked him to justify his existence. I mean, I *know* that I have peace with God—as a fact. But I have yet to become the kind of person whose default setting is to live as though this *peace* is my reality. I still carry the impulses of war in my motivation to move, in my reactions to the imperfections of those I love, and in my tunnel-vision approach to achieving "good" goals at whatever cost.

Of the many stories about Jesus that confront my assumption that measurable success is the key to my survival, there's one about a perfume jar that I can't seem to shake. Seemingly important to each gospel writer, the story can be found in Matthew 26, Mark 14, Luke 7, or John 12. If you haven't heard it, it's the one where Jesus is sitting with some of his students and contemporaries. They're in the home of a man named Simon. Simon, the leper, to be clear. Some of the people at this gathering aren't fond of Jesus, as you'll find out later. At this moment, their contempt is in an acceptable display case—the pretense of caring about heresy. Soon enough, though, it takes on the form of bearing false witness against Jesus (talk about heresy) so that he can be murdered publicly.

This is the setting. So, during what I assume must have been a perfectly normal evening, a woman enters the scene. Strike one. *Presumably*, a woman with a strikingly immoral reputation. Strike two. You can imagine the looks of disgust on the faces of these perfectly-respectable-thank-you-very-much men. The woman walks over to Jesus with a very nice perfume jar. The kind you'd insure if you had insurance. And she breaks the jar, just to pour the whole thing out on Jesus' feet. Strike three. That's just poor stewardship.

The wise guys (in whose camp I'd be) offer up a pretty quick, well-reasoned rebuke. The disciple-turned-double-agent Judas is recorded saying something like: "What an irresponsible waste! You could've sold that jar and given the money to the poor." Perhaps the others mumble in agreement, scrunching their faces at the overwhelming smell of perfume, elbowing each other to make note of their solidarity with the critique. Perhaps another continues the tirade, making eye contact with Jesus, pointing in his direction: "Right? I bet that's *exactly* what this guy is thinking."

Jesus, surrounded by a common consensus—the kind of consensus that is *technically* in alignment with his ministry, mind you—decides to be brave. He doesn't pick up this virtuous, logical idea to use it as a weapon against this woman.

"Leave her alone," he replies, awkwardly dividing the room, placing himself on the side of the weeping, objectified woman. Then, he describes her CPA-disapproved act as "beautiful". Where these men saw nothing even remotely tolerable in this woman's presence, Jesus beheld beauty.

He proceeds to declare that what she did was of an immeasurable value. It was an anointing. A priestly action.

As far as he was concerned, this disreputable, harshly-critiqued woman had anointed him for his burial.

The story ends with Jesus making a pretty bold claim: "Wherever the gospel is preached throughout the world, what [this woman did] will also be told, in memory of her." Memory, interestingly, is the reason Jesus gives for a continual retelling of this event. So, it's rather unhelpful, I think, that the gospel authors give us almost no details about this woman. Funerals are done "in remembrance" of the deceased, and they tend to include obituary readings and personal testimonies to commemorate the life being mourned. What can we really do "in remembrance" of this woman, 2,000 years later? This story's all we have.

But, I remember another time Jesus spoke about doing something "in remembrance." Right before walking into the murderous plot of those he'd just infuriated, he broke bread and drank wine with his closest disciples. He told them he'd be dying soon. And he instructed them to regularly gather with this bread and wine "in remembrance" of him. The bread would represent his body, broken for, and alive in them. The wine, his blood, shed for their forgiveness and healing. We now call this *taking communion*.

In Jesus' way of thinking, remembrance isn't just an obituary reading each time people take the bread and wine. It is an embodied practice that takes into account the deep meaning of his death and resurrection. The remembrance is a recalling of an event, certainly, but not for the sake of intellectual space being filled with trivia. Remembrance is for the sake of the *present moment* being colored by the reality of what has occurred in the past.

In that same manner, I'd like to let the gospel be proclaimed to me in a way that remembers the woman who prodigally shattered an alabaster jar at Jesus' feet and found herself honored by him despite her notable lack of practicality. Something about her act of pouring a years' wages upon Jesus to anoint him for his burial was born of the Spirit, and preached the good news. She was filled with sadness, as John notes. Perhaps even shame. She was surrounded by voices of contempt vilifying her actions. The money could have been given to the poor. I'm sure Jesus would have been happy with that course of action, too. But she, despite all their words, is dignified by the loving gaze of Jesus. "Let her alone. . . . She has done what she could . . ."

The good news that is often preached to me and by me, speaks so much of "maximizing your potential" and other productivity precepts. The promise of prosperity is held like a carrot in front of those who have the most will-power, certainty, followers, financial security, and whatever else. We're so afraid that we will end up as potentials unrealized, that we'll waste our lives. We make mission statements, five-year plans, and systems to measure "success" for our lives. These are, in most cases, fueled by anxiety and shame. But we sanctify it, marrying it to our call to walk as "those who live by the Spirit of God," (Romans 8:14). Our anxiety, our resentment, and our shame about "making an impact" drive our actions, though we say we are acting "in Jesus' name". Soon enough, we don't necessarily need to live in response to the Spirit, because we have all the criteria to measure our decisions and find out whether they're useful or not.

Enter the woman with her perfume jar—the woman whose story will be preached "whenever the good news is proclaimed in the world." In comes the woman who I would so quickly rebuke for being "a bad steward."

And I'm confronted by the fact that the *one* voice who can tell me what is actually meaningful and impactful doesn't rebuke or write off the woman's actions. He uses his voice to honor her.

I think what Jesus saw there was an action born of what he called *poverty of spirit* (Matthew 5:3). He saw the sacrifice of a "broken and contrite heart" (Psalm 51:17). He saw somebody led by the Spirit of God. He recognized this responsiveness to God's Spirit as the only way to be sure life was well-lived, not wasted. The rebukes of the men at the table who demanded measurable success blinded them from seeing what Jesus saw: beauty. The mysterious, irresponsible, lavish actions of this woman, through Jesus, became good news.

I

THE BEDROCK OF
EXHAUSTION

"Nap Time"

Like a child, I cannot believe
The only critique I must receive:
"You are tired."

How could I be tired if I'm so restless
And there's so much left to do?
If I sleep, who will protect this
World I'm conquering for you?

So, I kick and scream
Because all I've yet to do in the light
Sticks like an invisible thorn in my side
As if you stood stranded, gravely
Awaiting the might of my arrival—

What I *might* have done
And still should do

And even if this story were true:
        that it's righteousness I desire to see,
It'd all fall apart right here,
        where I started shouting at you.

Yes, like a child, I cannot believe
The only critique I must receive:
"You are tired."

"The Name I'd Forgotten"

It's not like I woke up one day
Hell-bent on how I could betray
The hope I couldn't keep away
It was death by a million paper-cut blows
Turning dearest friends to foes—
One unnamed expectation at a time
As I refused to know you,
Preferring you'd have taken cues
From the portrait I painted before you
Said my name

It's not like I woke up the next
Heaven-sent on a mission to fall apart
And let tears water the soil I ignored
But you were there that day,
Unbewildered by
The well-drawn facade's falling sides,
Saying the name I'd forgotten—
The one over which I'd scribbled,
        with self-made redemption plans—

You were there,
Tenderly giving away
That forgotten name.

"Directionlessness"

That you'd grace or dignify
The wilderness in which I
Think myself so often
Lost
Is the scandal for which I vie:

A God I can touch, whose hand is on mine
Directionlessness overcome by
Your embarrassing lack of pride

Yes, it was I who would try
To build your house
In the places I knew you were not around.

Did you not cry
To hear the sound
Of hammer-and-nail toil on holy ground?

I only ask, because
It must be sad to see your child
Work as though the love you give
Is the "well done" at the end of the mile.

"For This Night"

I've struggled against all the weight of my lists
Trying to carry you home
But today I am hit by some alien risk
To unburden my weary soul

Yes, I tried to fight, get my motives right
Paying for what I'd never own

Thank God for this night, for I'm seeing the light
Is somewhere outside my control

"Our Dance"

The missing-ness of it all surfaced again
I asked, "Grief, do you have anything new?"

"No, but you do."

I suspect this will be our dance:
You lead; I age.

"Speak!"

What do I do
To the voices that pursue
This home I've made for you
In this body of mine?
What do I say
To the flies I can't swat,
Swarming sorrows, to keep
A reasonable smile ajar?
Am I to entertain
These dissonant refrains
These threats to the life I've gained
By receiving from you?

Forgive me, but lately
They're the loudest I hear,
Louder than any roar
You ought to use to protect me from fear

Forgive me, but lately
They don't seem set to destroy;
But vaguely good deeds
Assuring death, I'll avoid

And, trust me, I know you are gentle—
Bold and strong—
But I am tired of reasoning
With the maybes of this song

I need wilderness replies!
And the ministry of angels!

I need the shepherd to talk back,
To make this heart stable.

Overstimulation makes me feel like a failure
When I am supposed to be the
Steady one.
But why would I expect to be
Like a quiet stream in the desert
While I am not drinking water?

"Hard Work"

Wind filters through the patches
Of rarely green grass while
An impartial sunlight comes
Smiling on dirt and fence alike
All the while, my clenched jaw says
Something snide and imprecise to
Convince me of all I don't have time to do

And this Friday morning, all that is clear
Is the choice before me:
To give in to the work held
Tightly in these raised shoulders
Or the hard, hard work
Of letting them come down
Again and again

"Survival"

How deep does this solitary blood flow
Moving my feet toward all they seem to know
To keep my hands safe from scratches and burns
I might receive from other flesh and bone?
The isolation suite I carry down the trail
I have prized with possessive records and tales,
How I've avoided further scars and bruises by pressing on
With this loneliness that clears my hands of what it is to
    fail
I suspect an award will come
Nearing the end of this path I've run
But, if not, it is no matter,
For I will have avoided the hell
Of receiving help, of needing the wealth
Of a father by my side.
Yes, this—is how I've tried
To stay alive.

"Evening Walk"

I descend
No longer holier-than-thou on this hill
But holy, for knowing who will fulfill
This purpose—
It's the world-making difference between
Trying *to* be,
And trusting I *will* be
Lifted up

"Grieving the Lost Love of Loneliness"

I remember when I could fake it—
That I was a rational fanatic,
A certain breed holding to a smugly superior creed,
We'd stand up, all one of us,
Flaunting our mantra without speech:
        There is nobody for whom we have need.

When the wind sauntered in to rake the leaves
Piled over my chosen debris,
Resurfacing each desire underneath
The foundation unbeknownst to me,
The soliloquy-soaked stage
Was swept into the periphery.

And this lesson leaves a particular ache:
My love for loneliness has been betrayed
Now that my memories taste like you.
Even when your absence is my only cue,
I cannot ignore my need for your pursuit
When I am left to sit in a lonely room.

"Oh?"

It can only make sense in the tired soul
That gentleness is too great a chore:
Something I don't have the energy for.

Oh? So the depletion you now possess
Will do better to face the fire you'll set
When you decide you cannot dress
Your words in the simple garments of gentleness?

"Vanity"

The vapor
Of my labor
For that which I surmise
I will only one day describe
Once and for all

A vapor,
You called it?
Yes, a vapor:
Made of that for which I thirst,
Yet not nearly enough
To satisfy.
So, when the rat race is run
I collapse,
Without enough water
For the tears I wish to cry—
All because I tried to drink
A vapor.

A vapor,
You called it?
Yes, a vapor,
Or a chasing after the wind,
Rightly describing
What I've come to recognize:
The thin clouds of resentment,
This body found running on fumes—
All because I tried to drink
A vapor.

"I'm Trying To Help You (And Other Lies I Tell Myself)"

If I had known
The rope I'd thrown
To rescue you from the pit
Served more like a whip,
Drawing blood where it was sent,
I'd give up this heart of stone.

But I can't yet see that far
When vision blurs red
With the memory of each scar
I only end up passing along
Under the guise of charity.

Perhaps with vision blurred red
My greatest task is not the
Ironclad, white-horse riding
Chivalry I believe it is, but
That of a visitor who just arrived
In a strange land:
To set my feet upon the ground, and
Slow down long enough to understand.

"Paralyzed"

You walked through my house while I was paralyzed,
Sat down beside me with no words of advice,
Listened to my barely-formed words through patient eyes,
And didn't say a word until sunrise.

It felt all too foolish to repeat this again:
For me to list all the places you hadn't been
For me to look straight through the eyes of a friend
And long for one to save me from the mess I was in

But you tested all my questions, unstandardized
Not to disprove my values, but to no longer let them me
    tell lies
Until none of my insecure answers would suffice
And all I had to look at were your patient eyes

"Depression"

I've sparred with a man called Depression
And I'm sure we're bound to meet again, see
What they won't tell you about this old friend
Is at some point, you've got to let him in

You'll know when the boards start breaking,
After years spent nailing them to your door,
That your will is no match for the time rolling past
The boundaries of your ideals' shore

You'll know when your own voice tapers,
After years of its wit like a shield,
That the borders you make are the gray bars you shake
Crying out for what you can't feel

"Forty-Two Seven"

I am in the water
Who remains under the wind
I will stay until currents flow
Unto the deeper floors or distant shores

I am eroding, resting, moving,
Subject to the form with which you surround me—
And let it be so, always

"Lessons From A Trembling Dog"

I've seen all my efforts fall
Vainly into the concrete ground
Below my feet, often enough
To say I'm open to figuring out
Whether the strength of my technique
Is really the stuff
The good life is made of, when

This dog shakes at the sound of thunder
And my words are no medicine at all
My hands might as well be fleas
Circling aimlessly with a purpose the rest of creation
Doesn't care enough to notice or ask about, recalling

What I've heard a thousand times,
From best friends and my beloved:
Trying to get power just might be
My only waste of precious time

II

TENSIONS TO ACCEPT

"It Must Be"

Sure, you know me,
        but how do I know
You haven't used
        the magnifying glass
I wield when wanting to know
Whether something appeals
To my gold standard?

Well, I guess it goes something like the fact
That you part seas before forming comebacks
After all my lackluster trust that I've called personality
I guess it must be, through love, that you know me.

"Unwinding"

You embrace the sinner,
You touch the heart of the saint,
You fear no loss of power,
Your love is what makes you great.

Stretched between tensions that don't exist,
Like law and grace,
Devotion and embrace,
I'm seeing

You are not the places in which I hoped,
Yet in them, you make a way.
You are not the people for whom I longed,
Yet you remain with them always.

"Timesheets and Seasons"

Is it time to bless or to retreat?
Maybe the question itself
Is the one who's lying.

For where do times come from
But the undivided heart
Whose value system seems to take no part
In the balancing act that calls
Any minute, who isn't followed
By captionable material, a waste?

Yes, I understand
We do not want to hoard,
But splitting hairs won't yield the joy
Of returning to the source.
And timesheets can't create
What only seasons can explain:
Light touches both fruitful field and barren plain;
And all that receives it cannot labor in vain.

"Soil and Concrete"

The difference I'm beginning to see
Is that of a building and a tree
Where barren ground had either to be met
With blueprints practically outstretched
Or seeds buried in trust and doubt

The first, so that the planner might give, then get
A reward from the world on which he'd bet
Hiring hands alone to craft a space
To house his longed-for human race

All the while, arms stretch from the seeds
Great and necessary processes going unseen
While the planter participates and observes
Inviting faces to enjoy her soil-driven work

And the latter grows with branches and leaves and fruits
Without the agenda drawn by those qualified by suits
Not flourishing because it was remodeled and coerced
But only by receiving the water of its thirst

And someday it may come that the tree is chopped down
By someone in search of the life they haven't found
But do not fret, you under its shade,
For it has lived by giving itself away
Though its place may fill with concrete
It is no threat to what you cannot see

Underground beauty labors in love
And your children's children will see life spring

"Shhhhh"

Sorrow, I'll take—
As it comes in waves
To throw me upon the shore.

But *shhhhh*
Shame, I will not bear—
For it wills not to share
In the joys it cannot afford.

For sorrow, my heart pounds,
My vision slows down,
Till I can see face-to-face.

But shame threatens to bury me,
Till I am what I am carrying.
So, let sorrow its place erase.

"Young and Old"

In the letdown-ness of my tired soul
Continues a conversation between young and old
Never is it what I'd expect
The wise man born yesterday knows never to mirror
The survival methods of the withering away
Who spent their lives serving this bondage to decay

Wisdom comes with age, so they say,
And I believe I can't know much until I reach coming days
But if age should deny the eternity set inside
The heart it tries so hard to keep alive,
Then the old would compartmentalize,
And avoid death by drawing lines,
Until a beauty like the sunrise seemed a waste of time

And I've grown cold enough to see
These methods I'm bound to repeat
So, even with war inside of me
Christ, come speak tenderly

"Gentleness and Power"

If I did not know
The gentleness of God
Yet still tried on his power
Well, I'd miss the latter altogether
In an eerie, flowerless Spring

No, it wouldn't take long
To realize something's off—
A slight temperature shift
Without the agreement of the soil
Budding with colors that mark the end of cold toil

We'd call it a lie,
A false start at best,
We'd wait for one to come
Who could grant Summer's request
To renew the ground and make a way
For the coming of unending days
Not being fooled merely by heat,
Void of the life-giving power of gentleness

"Maps and Tapestries"

Why is it so hard not to forget
I don't want what I want?
The looking glass to avoid storied past
Always leaves the seer more frenzied than free.

What does it say of me
That I believe my life to be
A matter of topography,
A map rather than a tapestry?

No, answers, it is not you I seek
At least, not any longer.
What you falsely guarantee, let me
Freely receive.

"Either Way"

Doesn't seem to matter much
Whether I'm enslaved or exiled
Both require rescue
And that's what you do

Doesn't seem to matter much
How clearly I hear your voice
Either way is seeking
Finding is the promise you're keeping

"Manipulative Humility"

If I could feign enough gratitude
For the way things are
I could convince the future
To no longer remain so far

Humbling myself in the name of pride,
Could I train you to think my vanity died?
I'd be the fool who finally figured you out
Along with every king who took this means-to-end route.

No, do not bow low
So you can call yourself a king!
For that path is fraught
With a sorrier suffering.

It is not for the future alone
That we delight in the now's small things,
But for the right-now love given to the literal least.

"Left-Handed Religion"

Left-handed religion
Nothing built is built for me
I don't fit in the test-taking seats
And it's not that I am your faith without deeds
But that I must respond to Love
Before the scorekeepers have their chance to see

So, when everyone comes out to measure my height
With the motives birthed under influence of fright
I'm home, less alone, asleep in my bed
Learning to trust the secret place instead

"Naming the Narrowness"

The narrowness of the road—
That holds the life I cannot name,
All I desire yet know not how to claim—
Is not due to the one by whom it is paved,
But like all trails surrounded by trees
Overgrowth crowds the path with leaves
Rarely stepped on or over.

Many choose not to tread on the grass
Growing back throughout the lonely path.
There are many others with much clearer bends
That we can ignore until we reach their ends.

There are many roads nearby, acquainted with self-defense
Calling the overgrown path an enemy of common sense.
And of course! Their critique is sound.
For the sense most common is to leave oneself unbound
To the care of any results yet unseen,
And to call such misery "liberty"
For every result we've recorded is buried under the widest
    trails.

Despite its obscurity among the thorns
There are no gravesites to polish along the path we scorn.
Its sign so welcoming, it deters us all:
"Live no longer bracing for your own fall;
Commit to your reception, before death's unwelcome call."
So reads the road—only made narrow by the deception of
    regret.

"Explanation and Yearning"

I think I found out what scares me
About that Great Return
It's my trying to explain it
More than letting myself yearn

See, I want to be found blameless
Yet I want to be found heard

But I guess that's what you meant—
Talking to me about the other birds
One leads to the other
Not in the order I understand

Yes, I can know you long before I know
The blueprints of your plans

"Potential"

A creed was preached in that Physics classroom
And then again, for days on end
Until Summer came to bloom

Potential, potential, the energy whose value
Only tomorrow's power could prove
So it ever remained, theoretically substantial
I had so much, and I'm sure
You had so much, too
To this day, the prophesied movement, our muse
All of us marked—
       as not quite yet kinetic
       full of potential, like plans made on credit
Marveled at, but moreso, objectified
For the potential that lay dormant inside

I'm thankful for the knowledge,
       don't get me wrong
But could I raise my hand, challenge
       one of Newton's laws?
If we're all just messes of untapped resources,
Making dents on the earth and beating dead horses,
What sets us apart from the things that we build,
Who are full of potential:
Only useless when still?

"How Are You Strong?"

I always thought strength
Had to be accompanied
By an earth-shattering list of feats
Like the mighty breakers of the sea
Who live in such harmony
Until, on occasion, they yield tragedy
As if giving back the saltwater abundance
Supplied to them by our tears

But that seems more like groaning
In junction with all created things
Melding our scraps of sorrow into weapons of war
Because we've yet to remember what we're longing for:
The piercing whisper of The Poet's voice
Sitting unafraid, above the waves
Because love is his only choice

How are you jealously,
Zealously committed to my betterment,
Without standing over me, holding
Some cruel master's whip?

How do you love without fear
That I will not hear
And take the easy route of
Making me your project?

How are you unashamed
That I have been named
Your brother—your friend?

I keep looking for you above, hovering
But you are nowhere to be seen
How do you walk right next to me
Exchanging violence for a desperate lover's plea?

"The Gate on The Way to the Park"

On the way to the park—
Why did they put up that gate I can always walk around?
To keep out the machinery
From committing the thievery
Which it is all about?
Whereby it steals my mind from the breeze
With its listless litany
Of spells for those who stand blankly spellbound

Yes, I guess
The gate is a humble protest, at best
But it is the humblest things
That welcome me
To ignore the un-humble humming sound
Of the created things
Who accuse my peace
Each time I keep them around

"When He Asked The Question"

When he asked the question
About adding minutes,
I raised my hand,
Certain I'd surpassed these limits
Certain my pacing was for the good of mankind
Certain my worry was no less than divine.

Then, a photo flashed before my eyes:
The dwindling peaks of a slowly beeping monitor, for the
    one
       who set their heart on mastering time, or
The tsunami's waves crashing down
      upon sandcastles and smiles.

And I was certain that worry,
My cell-mate friend—
Was child of the same spirit
Of every earthquake I couldn't end;
A groan in the wrong direction
Seeking to preserve all my youth
When those closest to perfection
Grow old hand-in-hand with truth.

All I'm trying to say is: To worry is to prepare for death by
    trying to overwrite it,
rather than learning to embrace it as the non-end that it has
    become.

III

LEARNING TO BREAK
A PERFUME JAR EVEN
THOUGH DOING SO WILL
UNDOUBTEDLY MAKE YOU
SEEM UNSUCCESSFUL OR
UNFAITHFUL

"Goodness, No"

A good thing is
A fragile thing
Quickly dismantled,
Demurred, disarmed of its original picturesque beauty.
Cracks develop in the safety of
The roads we pave
To be spotless, temporary homes
To travelers and tires.
All the while, what is good,
What blesses our sights and bodies—
The growing grass sprouting from the soil
Develops between the cracks in the road
Because the fragile, good thing
Had a goodness underneath
And goodness, no—
Goodness, is a fragile thing

"On Softening"

Why am I doing this—
Out here, giving myself away
So un-calculated, so freely
So that the slightest bump in the road
Is permitted to evoke
A waterfall of tears?

"The Kids"

Will I ever feel fruitful?

We could talk it through again—
The towel around your waist,
The road contouring your face,
And the vineyard I long to understand.

I'll hear out this idea,
This echo undermining
Every voice amplified by almost-silver lining
Fitting in like a cool wind
Against this desert sandstorm,
Saying something about forgiveness
And something about the kids
Who do not climb the same mountains
We climb to take all that we give

No, they jump head-first
Into the arms that bend
Around all their weaknesses
To un-condemn and bandage
The words that aren't hidden

Their story knows a glory
All desire to re-live
But none desire to accept:
A barefoot way, though shoes can stay
And still, I fail to trust
I must be given what I long to gain

"God Won't Be Praised"

God can't be praised
By the defenses I raise,
The walls I've tattooed with his name
Not a vision or plan, like a battering ram
Held by my fists of rage

He might just be the one I hit
With all my best ideas
Taking out my guns, one by one
Trying to set my iron will free
While the prison cell I locked him in
Becomes the place I long to be

No, God won't be praised
By the defenses I raise,
Trying to protect my own name
So, come tear them down,
Till I'm left unafraid
In the presence of a love that won't change

"The House"

The only way
To answer the age-old question:
Have I labored in vain?
Is to survey the house
To which your efficiencies amount
And see if, in its many rooms
Love dwells.
If not, you have your answer.

"Glory"

The thing about glory is
It's a heavy thing
I've gloried on mountaintops
With vision so clear and free
The whole world felt like
A small and lovely thing

But what of the heaviness
Of glory being this dazzling light?
What of the space and time in which
We find all vision is blurred,
Ghosts whisper but remain unheard,
And we cannot name a thing?

The question I really have is:
Am I now blind *to* your glory,
Or being blinded *by* it?

"Well-Meaning"

Many well-meaning men may have tried to remove Christ
    from the cross,
But at what cost?
The discomfort of suffering temporarily erased, in one
    place
To avoid, once more, the burden of loss

I am that well-meaning friend,
In the ashes,
Looking down at Job

Free me to enter those
Unfixable sorrows

"(Incomplete)"

Life is not a problem
My soul, know it well
Life is no more a problem
Than out-of-tune wedding bells

"Stretched"

Now I tell myself I am being stretched
Where what used to be easy feels like a test
And stubborn as I am,
I have to believe it was my plan
For it to happen at all

But the plan was not mine
And that's what is so divine
About being stretched.

"The Fear of Being Unqualified for Help"

Do you mourn for me, Friend,
Like you know it all too well?
The nervous sound of the in-between
Ringing like an empty bell

I can't seem to shake it
And I've worn out my best words
Now, nothing's left, so my best guess
Is to tell you where it hurts

But if the other souls you spoke to
By bandaging their wounds
Had it worse than this small curse
Will I see you change your tune?

Will you laugh at me, Doctor,
For thinking I qualified
To be healed through this appeal
When "*technically, not everything*" has been tried?

See, I've grown small just thinking
I could raise my hand for help
Only once I'd lost enough
That I couldn't help myself

So, mourn for me, Friend, for
I'm quite sure I don't know how
And I'll fall apart, to see your heart
Be broken by mine now

"The Fearless Kind of Fear"

Fear is no thing that has made me wise
Well, except for that funnily fearless kind
That gently breaks in—to blind my eyes
From every heedless word of advice
They've heaved at me in order to supply
Whatever they've learned will satisfy
That beast who demands I merely survive
Until I am unknown by such battle cries
And thrown wholly upon what will suffice
So that even when the accuser can't be denied
It is no longer invited to the trial of the unjustified

"Nice Try"

You are not love.
Where love, to me, would say: "Do not be afraid,"
You exercise too much restraint
Once the wheels of anxiety spin,
Saying:
"You've probably got a point."

"Save Your Breath"

"I could've done better,"
I say to myself
Reflecting on earlier today,
The appointment I betrayed,
The remark I made

"I could've done better"
Is a useless breath of air
For the "I" to which I direct
The accusation was not there
And though he's but a few hours different
Than I, looking back,
I could've done better
Than placing him under attack.

If there are invites
For reparations to be made,
Do not stand unforgiving
In the waters you used to wade.
"I could've done better"
Is so often a weapon, merely
Taking on humility's shape.

"Tie-Dye"

At what point does the stain become the dye,
Re-working what lay originally inside
The garment?

Can it ever be lifted?
Or is it now redeemed by
A stain-inspired tie-dye
Unlike anything yet seen?

"Dead Dreams"

I'm scared to bring back
The dreams I bullied
And hear what they have to say

It was for good reason,
Their danger to my heart,
I kept their ambitions at bay

Still, I cannot help but feel
Their tugging upon my shirt
As I wake up, or go to sleep
In the house built atop their place in the dirt

If they are resurrecting
There's no sense in self-defending
For they'll only bless me to my core
But, how can I know
They're not just ghosts
Come back to steal what I adore?

No, I cannot bear
The weight of this decision
Call it wisdom, call it superstition,
But I am scared to give open seats
To what I thought were better-dead dreams

I don't know!
Is it better to let them sit
And say their piece, even if it won't fit,
So they can meet the host

They used to outbid,
And stand in awe of his will to forgive?

"Leafless"

Do you resent this tree,
No longer bearing leaves
Standing tall, across from one whose continue to grow?

Or do I shortsightedly
Issue such fixated decrees
That *I* forget what *you* must know?

These branches have not given up,
　　　have not bitterly labored in vain.
No, subtle winds have carried all their losses
　　　to needful, empty plains.

And I suppose the evergreen
　　　will be unto me shade,
As I recall—leafless trees
　　　are resurrections displayed.

"A Well-Lit Room"

There is a flame, burning bright
There is a room, covered in light
There is no need for soul to hide
There is a safety, unwelcoming to lies

I am false, but not despised
Where I'm true, you aren't surprised
I am afraid, but judgment dies
Where I'm too weak to supply
A shield to save me from this great light

"Frequency"

It comes in waves
But it comes more often
As the questions who surface
Are more asked than forgotten

It comes in waves
But it comes more often:
Alignment of spirit,
Of body, of soul
With the love that draws me
Far beyond my control
Alignment of thought,
Of sense, of each breath
With the unmeasured grace
That won't leave me for dead

It comes in waves,
But it will come more often.

"Debt"

What a gift
To forever be indebted
To one who deeply enjoys
Paying my bills

"Anxiously"

I thought I would let the world know
You are with me
Anxiously

But it was only when
I sat long enough
To let you wash the dirt
Off my feet
That the message I preached
Carried a smile I couldn't teach
Myself when I tried to bless
Through anxiety

IV

PRAYERS THAT ARE
INCONSISTENTLY HONEST

"On Being A Mountain"

From one mountain to another
The view up here is snow-capped,
Levels below serene
Now that these eyes are made
Scanning, unwelcoming, you see

At least for the brick wall
There's the chance of the bulldozer who
Recognizes your stubbornness, finally
Knocking you over

But here, with my head in the clouds,
Like the other mountains taught,
I can't be shaken, so I'll request
The help of the one who said
Mountains could be thrown
Into the sea
To learn humility

"Thanksgiven"

Of my breath,
Which flows more slowly as my eyes close,
I can say very little,
Without saying "thank you"
For as long as it goes.

Of my breath,
Which animates the self I often inflate,
I know very little,
Without first knowing
It is given.

"Escaping Grace"

Voice against my reason, carefully shattering my pride,
If I could escape you, I'm no longer sure I'd try.

When I swim back from ocean depths
        to manageable shorelines,
Your whisper goes beyond the waves
To become the silence in which I hide.

Hands that built the fire
Whose flames consumed my dreams,
If I cannot see your touch where sunlight kisses sea,
Whether I turn my head and fail to meet you in my
    memory,
It is still so,
        that you've never crafted flames in vain.
So, may this emptiness bear
        witness to belief.

Why would I escape you, after all that I've been told,
Unless the reason for my running
        was to see you break the mold,
Keeping me from knowing you?

"Flying Lesson"

I wonder why
These birds spend so much time on pavement
Choosing to fly only when
They forget where safety went

I want to befriend
My weightlessness in the wind
More than I peck at breadcrumbs on the ground

And when I touch ground
Share the love I have found
Where the heavens couldn't seem to end

"Precious"

To be precious
To be cared for
Looked after, not by a hired hand
In need of payment
But held by hands
Who have taken the time
To know and work with
The jagged edges and scratched
Faces of the rough diamond
That is my soul

Carried always
In thought and deed,
Enjoyed, smoothed out,
And polished for good
Often and when needed

"That Noise"

The hours, days, years I've spent—
Scratching, searching, screaming, seething
In anger at that noise
Like a flea around my head,
An intruder in the basement
Of my perfectly-well-kept-thank-you-very-much
Heart—

All come into view, making sense
As the shoes come off
The ground hallowed by my finally curious
Heart

That terribly annoying sound
Oh, it was you, all along
Knocking at the door with the grief
My signs against solicitors rejected
Now I'm ready for
The hope you're selling
Break down the door, for all I care
This isn't a poem anymore;
I mean it right now
Flood the house if you've got to, please
Anything is better than the sting of
Making sure you never got past my porch

"The Beggar"

When should I finally
Believe how you approach me
With power used so mildly
I'll likely hide my face?

For it is a shameful
Scandal in my eyes
To see a king beg for bread or wine.
Yet where our stories unbreakably intertwine
Is where you cry aloud with hunger and thirst.

I'm sorry, the markets have taught me well:
"God helps those who help themselves."

So, forgive unforgiving me
Until these taut eyes always see
God, The Beggar,
Turning famine to feast.

"Moving"

Would it be possible
To finally sit down
Among the broken-down and still-full boxes,
No longer listening to the siren song:
"Just one more, then we'll be done,"
Take off our shoes,
Make the moment our muse,
Just long enough to call this new place "home"?

"Some Gift"

Life is the kind of gift God gives
The vibrant, growing, sleeping, laughing kind
The kind that will break down the walls of your city
More often than it stands watch on top of them
Only to show you the giver also lives outside.

Will you receive it?

"The Time Comes"

I mean, it must happen to us all, right?
And I'm not sure it has much to do with maturity,
More than it has to do with skids and suffering.
But all I'm saying is, the time comes.

The time comes, and we may choose to reject
The realization of our unsustainable methods to self-protect.
The time comes for each each one of us
To see the way we've kept our heads above water:
Treading with arms that will, one day, too tired grow
Standing on the backs of those who learned to breathe
    below,
And we will say to ourselves, to the heavens above, either
"What would it be for me to be fully immersed?"
Or "I've stayed alive, haven't I? What's another year of
thirst?"
While around our curiosity, the living water stirs,
Slowly asking the question to all under this tiring curse.

"Some Hymn"

This is your song
I've no strength to sing
Your weakness is strong
When I feel nothing

No hint of the wind
Parting the seas
No grand invitation
To dress up and feast

No triumphant shout
Like a rock for my feet
No, still this your song
The weakness of need

The crying, "my God,
Did you just leave me?"
The fear met with silence
The searchlight I can't see

This is your song
In darkness I'm free
Your weakness is strong
When I feel nothing

"Ascent"

Oh, Jesus, if I make it past my mockery
Stare long enough, uncomfortably,
At your arms, outstretched, unmoving,
I feel your embrace

Oh, Jesus, if I give up eliminating mystery
I may find myself on Calvary
And through weeping eyes, see finally
Our Father's face.

"Unprayed Prayers"

Before words
Like petition and intercession and contemplation,
Unspoken prayers form
In the child's heart—
A longing for Zionlike steady souls
To surround and uphold

And it is those unprayed prayers
With unmade answers,
Swirling in the mess of this
Taller child's heart,
For which I find it hurts to imagine
A world of anything more than
Coincidence and chance

So now that I have words, I ask
For hope

"A Letter"

Carry me, in wind and hail
Deserted and forlorn
Around your shoulders, till I jump
Upon the absence of conflict in the air
Only to find that my lonely mastery of time
Was a myth that whipped up the storm

Carry me, whether or not I've failed
To keep my need before my eyes
In the places I can't see
My healing is in the holding on
So, carry me.
Carry me.

"Let Me Be"

If it is true:
That nothing will bend,
Then let me be—
Gladly in what is
No longer possessing the futile strength of distress
To straighten out one inch
Of a whole world being made whole

"Steady"

Steady the waves under the wind
Steady the sun upon my skin
Steady the longing placed within
Exposed to behold all over again
That my feet would rest on soft shores
That my hand would gently surround yours
That my eyes would close to plot no course
That my heart would settle in hopeful remorse
To once and for all become
Steady

"On Curing"

It takes some time
Spiraling, rejoicing, reprising, circling
Till I have eyes to see
The drain I've been circling 'round
Is the same mountain
On which I can usually be found

The shivering cold I have acknowledged
Yet forgotten how to wear
The peak, taunting in the distance,
Met by my longing-for-warmth-stare
All along, my jacket,
Never enough to fight this air

Riddled with the rumors
Of the men who have hurt
My soul that has grown
In spite of, and because of, their words

Whispering with its icy touch
Of the mysteries, I do not think enough
Because I would love nothing more
Than once and for all to call its bluff
And say I have solved the mess I've seen:
The tireless ache to be unseen
Yet known entirely, and
Understood by the
Dumbest and wisest, and in between

To speak words of substance
To this, altogether loveless
Fear inside your armored chest
Of your spiraling, rejoicing, reprising, circling life
I am working on a cure

But my climbing daily shatters my strategy
And I can't stop ascending
So, I must stop defending
My efforts to reclaim
The ground that I've lost
Entering this world's birth pangs

That will not respond to my technique
So, this, my prayer,
My fist-through-the-wall plea:
To stand at the door of my heart and yours
And extend a steady hand into the mystery

"Your Patience Fails Me"

Good men have told me so much I no longer believe
And bad men have talked me down, so all I've got is me
And I don't know which one I am, no, I can't hold the sea
So if there's someone drowning in it, come and rescue me

I've lost the will to balance myself, lost the will to think
I've lost my sense of wondering what everything means
Do you think I might still qualify as someone who is free
If all that used to hold me up has been replaced by need?

I've been preaching to myself that there's nothing I need
And I know I meant well, but now I can't stand poverty
So fill me in, or let me win by falling underneath
'Cause your patience fails me every time success is calling

"Realignment and Reckoning"

This may be more of a realignment than a reckoning
Both bear certain difficulties
But I might be more at ease with reckoning, for at least

Everybody sees
While you walk down the mountain
Shattered into a million pieces
Of stardust, finally glowing,
To be placed again among the
Night sky from which you fell
For at least, everybody sees
And will not let it slip your mind
Until you cannot forget you are tasked
With defying gravity

The trouble that comes from realigning
Is I've no mountain to descend
I've no revelation to spend
Days relaying to every ghost and friend
So, rather than a task ahead like church bells ringing
Or a chorus of angels in front and behind
My body will know, by the way I'm sitting
If I am now aligned

ACKNOWLEDGMENTS

This collection of poems wouldn't be possible without the kindness of family and trusted friends who continue along the Way with me. You have blessed, encouraged, rejoiced, and wept with me. You have pretended to care about poetry. I'll keep going until you tell me to quit it.

Many of these poems were included in other publications who were gracious enough to share them. Thank you to *Ekstasis Magazine*, *Solid Food Press*, *Clayjar Review*, *Calla Press*, and *Agape Review*.

Jen, we're only getting started on the best part.

All praise and gratitude to the Father, the Son, and the Holy Spirit. I have been, am being, and will be found by the One who is before all things and in whom all things hold together. Thank you for continually meeting me in the places where I do not imagine you will be.

ABOUT THE AUTHOR

 Despite being named after the greatest professional basketball player of all time, Jordan Sleed bravely sacrificed his surefire NBA career to begin writing. Though the world mourned, this shift came as no surprise to his friends and family. The San Antonio native has always had a soft spot for the contemplative life. And whether through prose, music, or poetry, he would confess that the discipline of putting pen to paper has been a source of spiritual subsistence—a means of encountering grace, making meaning, and prayerful connection with God and others.

His first collection of poetry, *The Rage Against Grace*, emerged when he began to be deeply troubled by the question: "What if the things I'm supposed to let go of are *good* things?"

Jordan is a musician, spiritual director, and pastor in San Antonio, Texas. He and his (much) better half, Jen, live in Texas, where they walk their dogs, love their friends, and do the dishes. You can probably find him underlining everything in a Henri Nouwen book, watching tennis, or needlessly analyzing a Stevie Wonder chord progression.